Seventy-One DAYS

HOW TO SAY GOODBYE
WHEN DEATH SAYS HELLO

A Caregiver's Guide

Seventy-One DAYS

HOW TO SAY GOODBYE
WHEN DEATH SAYS HELLO

A Caregiver's Guide

Karla L Booker, MD

Extreme Overflow Publishing

Dacula, Georgia

ISBN: 979-8-9881497-9-8

For permission requests, contact the publisher.

Extreme Overflow Publishing

A Brand of Extreme Overflow Enterprises, Inc

P.O. Box 1811, Dacula, GA 30019

www.extremeoverflow.com

Send feedback to info@extremeoverflow.com

Printed in the United States of America

Library of Congress Catalog in-Publication

Data is available for this title

To those who feel like they're drowning in the deep seas of grief,
rest assured that the tide has turned.

TABLE OF CONTENTS

ACKNOWLEDGEMENTS

How can I write this book, this guide through grief for a caretaker, without acknowledging Kent Allen Pindle Smith. Sunrise, March 6, 1962. Sunset, January 6, 2015. You taught me everything I needed to know; to live this life full, wide open, and intentionally, all about the pursuit of happiness. I'd say I miss you, but I don't. Because you're right here.

Secondly, I have to acknowledge my loving husband, Kenneth Dwain Strickland, who just is the husband I'm supposed to have for the rest of my life. You picked me right up and hold me steady. You believe in me, like, honestly, no one else ever has. Thank you for supporting me through this and believing that this story needed to be told. Thank you for your selflessness in understanding that I don't have to stop loving one man in order to love another. And it makes all the difference.

PREFACE

Death.

The Final Frontier.

Or is it?

Death is thought of as a place where one ceases to exist. The disappearing of one's self is the ultimate loss of control. Add to that the fear of non-existence, nothingness, and all the boogey monsters we fear hide beneath our beds. Grief turns into our worst fears of the unknown. We can't help but terrify ourselves when we don't know what's next. But what if we could flip our inherent thoughts about death completely upside down? What if we could gain control of our sanity during grief and, in turn, our lives by shifting our perspective about what happens to us after our faces are no longer visible to others? What if we could experience a sensation that no longer holds our breath hostage? A true exhale. What if, after the death of a loved one, we gifted ourselves the freedom to live, risk, and chase adventure? To create opportunities to experience joy…to love again. Would you grab hold of that opportunity?

The greatest spiritual books of our time describe a life that is full to overflowing. A joyful and abundant life where we are not just allowed but are encouraged to untether ourselves from the dock, to unfurl our sails, and catch the wind. Even in the experience of grief.

Losing a spouse can be one of life's most difficult experiences. The pain, sorrow, and sense of loss can be overwhelming and last for years. While the grieving process is unique to each individual, and there is no one right way to deal with the emotions that come with it, I solicit you to consider death, grief, and love as one.

In this book, I ask you to boldly explore the different spaces of grief in which you may find yourself. It's easy to get stuck, so let's take this opportunity to get ahead of it! For those who feel you're already stuck, trust that reading this guide is the first step in getting 'unstuck.' Together, we will delve into grief's emotional and physical effects, providing insight into coping with the pain and gently moving forward into your new normal.

By holding this guide in your hands, you're taking the first step in your grief journey to wholeness. Bravo!

INTRODUCTION

*Courage— it's from the Latin word cor, meaning heart
— and the original definition was to tell the story of who you
are with your whole heart.*

— Brené Brown

Welcome to this chapter in your life. I know you would never have chosen it, but here you are. No matter what phase of this journey you're on: hit with this new diagnosis, in the midst of treatment, discussing hospice, or dealing with the physical loss of your loved one, you're not alone. I am here for you and celebrate your courage to walk this journey of grief with intentionality.

Myriad research shows that the journey through grief has stages, which are fluid – without limits of time or order. This journey is personal to you and your history. The most painful parts of the journey will last as long as you allow them to. I know it feels like you have no choice – you've been sucked into a nightmarish version of your life story. But I promise that shifting this perspective from passive to active will pull you forward in a way that nothing else will.

Let's be real – sometimes pain is so familiar and 'natural' that it feels kind of good just to let it stay and wash over you. Until it doesn't. The actual shift into grieving happens when you move from being a character in a tragic love story to being a real woman who has lost her life partner, her romantic lead...her best friend.

The Great Love Story. Everyone wants one. The Princess Tiana, Ariel, Snow White, Cinderella Disney love story. "My life was so bad, and then he came and swept me away – and now life is a fairytale!" All of that. It really did feel like that for me. My favorite cousin, who knows me best, says that this love story had to be a big, overreaching, all-consuming fairytale for my bruised little heart to believe it actually happened.

I came to this great love at 51 years old, a confirmed bachelorette and divorcee who had given up on the idea of a lifetime love. He changed all that. The painful shift into grieving was an un-tethering myself from the fairytale of a great love. A great love that I thought I'd lost.

The evolution of my grief journey continues to unfold

even as I write today. I write because of him. Kent Smith was my first love.

We were in Mrs. Zanders' fifth-grade class at Lucas Valley Elementary School in San Rafael, California. I believe I loved him long before that! Third grade, it was. He was my brother's very best friend. The eldest of five brothers, whose names all started with a 'K.' Our mothers were the best of friends. The best part was that I got to be 'Wendy' to this passel of 'Lost Boys,' hopelessly in love with Peter Pan.

My home was chaotic and fragile. It was built on a 1960s marriage between two people who really did love one another but didn't have the courage to step away from their own cocoons to marvel at the wondrous transformations of the other. The other perceived every shift and move and bit of growth as a rejection, a pulling away. And they punished one another for it. Over and over again.

And then there was Kent. In my household, which existed veiled by layers of fear and unrest, he championed me time after time. Kent, whose smiling eyes found mine no matter where we were, made me feel like the most perfect little girl ever created. He moved away after fifth grade to Richmond, Virginia, where my grandmother lived. The next time I saw him was in the seventh grade when anyone around us knew that we were hormonally mad for one another. Each summer, my grandmother let me see 'those Smith Boys' just one time. Bliss.

Fast forward to college. It was my Freshman year at Hampton, and Kent was at Howard. He was throwing the most excellent party in DC, and my brother, Jimmy, delivered Kent's invitation to me. We had the most wonderfully romantic and freely sexual weekend together. Thoughts of it still make me blush some forty years later. However, I had aspirations of a medical career and felt that marriage and medicine were mutually exclusive terms. The mixing of these thoughts carried my life into varied phases of chaos and confusion and kept me uncommitted and afraid. I became the most confirmed and unapologetic bachelorette I'd ever met.

In 2013, 32 years later, the majesty of Facebook changed the trajectory of my life forever! There was this picture of him, posting that he was smoking his last cigarette! That face, those eyes, drew me in, and the same blush overtook me once again. I replied to his post about how brave he was to be quitting after 30 years, and then there was a response about how proud my husband and I must be at the marriage of our daughter. I corrected that, though proud, I was not married! There was a pause, and he said, "I'm on my way!" to which I replied, "Come on!" It was surreal. And you want to know what? I could feel that he really was ON HIS WAY to me.

We fell. There's no other way to describe it. Wait. Let me be pristine in my telling of this tale. Falling implies some sort of accidental event. That is inaccurate. We saw the edge, recognized the joy on the other side, grasped hands, and dove, unfettered by our fears and insecurities, believing 'we' were the answer to life's every question. And you know what? We really were.

Ninety-nine days after a stage 4 lung cancer diagnosis with brain metastasis, Kent Allen Pindle Smith left the realm of life as we know it. It's been eight years, and I can still hear his wretched snoring, which was the lullaby to my slumber for those blessed 20 months.

Seventy-one days was the number of days Kent was my wedded husband.

I remember the Thursday night we decided to get married. Kent had been re-admitted to the hospital with excruciating pain in his affected lung and was being prepped for surgery. I said, "Babe, I think we should go ahead and get married. How about Monday?" Through a haze of pain meds, he said, "Ok, Puddin'. I'll marry you on Monday." Smiles and kisses were followed by prayers for healing and a good surgical outcome. Those prayers were tested, as Kent could not come off the ventilator immediately after surgery and went into septic shock that night. I remained at his bedside, praying Psalms 139 over him... 'Even the darkness will not be dark to you; the night will shine like the day, for darkness is as light to you.'

Faithfully, God showed out as He is known to do, and we married on that Monday.

When I began planning the wedding with my ever-watchful mommy, she asked me why I decided to do this. I think her biggest concern was that it would be such a financial burden completely on my shoulders. Knowing that our legal papers were in order, giving me all the rights and authority of a wife, she wanted to know what difference it would make. I would still be able to care for him and be his life partner, so nothing would change. I explained that we were choosing one another. For us, the ultimate choice was making that commitment before God that this is my person. Marriage means that I will be your partner, as a covenant with God, for the rest of your life. And the rest of his life was 71 days.

I didn't focus on how many days he had left. I focused on making sure that every day that he did have left was the best day of his life.

My life with Kent had been so blissfully happy! For the first time, I felt consistently safe and fully self-expressed. I simply could not fathom a life without him. I felt anger, a secondary emotion fueled by the fear of being forced to do life alone – AGAIN. After he died, I tried everything to get rid of this anger and fear: to buy it away, eat it away, sleep it away, and dance it away. Coming from the perspective that my love was 'lost,' the weight of my grief, pain, and hurt just didn't go away.

Finally, after two years, when I was getting over being angry at God and began crawling back to Him, I was reading Sarah Young's fabulous "Jesus Calling" devotion and found this:

"Do not be ashamed of your emptiness. Instead, view it as an optimal condition for being filled with my peace."

I didn't really know that emptiness was a feeling. I had no concept that what I was feeling was empty until I read that devotion. Then it said, "Cry out to God all of your hurts." I cried out to God, "Why did you allow me to be abused? Why did my father leave? And why did you take Kent??!" I heard God say back, "You thought that if you had the love of a man, you'd have the perfect life. So, I gave you this 'perfect man' and his 'perfect love'. But you have to know that all of that perfect love was always Me [loving you through him] all along."

Before Kent's transition, I don't think I could have ever seen God the way that I see him now. BK – 'Before Kent,' I saw God through this veil of trauma, which showed Him as a strict disciplinarian but never as a loving Father. This view led me to unknowingly choose constant defensiveness and self-protection. I didn't understand it then, but I do now: This trauma perspective kept me from giving my heart generously. Trusting no one. For me, the world was a very angry and dangerous place, and the universe was simply not conspiring in my favor. This left a gaping hole that I tried to fill in all the 'worldly' ways. Going through this grief process taught me a new lesson, which has become a mantra: "Just because it doesn't feel good, doesn't mean it *isn't* good." This mantra saves me from myself day by day.

The Bible says that in God, there is no darkness at all, that He is all only light (1Jn 1:5). That means everything we see and experience really is only light. We just have to be willing to sift through all the feelings, pain, and chaos and find God's light. Are you willing? Are you with me?

Consider this: If there were no difficulties in life, we would never pray. If everything was always good, we'd have no need for Him.

This reminds me of my favorite movie, The Matrix. In The Matrix, the 'Smith' is interrogating Morpheus, and he says, "Did you know that the first Matrix was designed to be a perfect human world? Where none suffered, where everyone would be happy. It was a disaster. No one would accept the program. Entire crops were lost. Some believed we lacked the programming language to describe your perfect world. But I believe that, as a species, human beings define their reality through misery and suffering. The perfect world was a dream that your primitive cerebrum kept trying to wake up from. This is why the Matrix was redesigned to this: the peak of your civilization." Cue a picture of a city of desolation and destruction.

The machines tried to make a paradise world to keep us calm, asleep, and plugged in, but we inherently rejected all of that goodness and perfection. There has to be difficulty. There has to be a struggle. There has to be strife in this life, giving us something to fight for, something to work for. It's just human nature.

There is a "struggle" even in love. Love is not easy. And if it is easy, the Bible says it's not really love. [Matthew 5:46 AMP] We have to fight - we have to struggle for it.

Sometimes, the word fight morphs into 'being in sync with.' To STAND for something. Like, 'this is where I'm supposed to be, and this is the conversation I'm supposed to be having. This is the experience I'm supposed to be going through." And God sees it all! He sees the beautiful, forever love that's going to be made manifest by having us go THROUGH this struggle.

We're groomed by our culture to see death symbolized by darkness: cemeteries, ghosts, goblins, ghouls, and The Grim Reaper on Halloween. We have it that death is something to be feared. As if talking about it will unleash the power of darkness, and something bad will happen! You know you've felt this! This is a pervasive yet dangerous way for us to look at the physical death of a being. As a society, across socio-economic norms, we're all raised to experience death in this way, using the words LOSS, ABANDONMENT, BEING LEFT BEHIND... A MISSING.

Another consideration: What if death is just a new iteration of life? What if death is just the next phase? This physical realm - in the grand scheme of forever. This flesh-to-flesh experience we have, in the grand scheme of all eternity, is just a sliver of time. Just a snap of our fingers! So, if this physical experience of life is merely a sliver of time, should it really be getting all of the emphasis and prioritization? In this way of thinking, DEATH – the end of our physical being – has no value and gets no credit.

If the laws of Physics are correct and matter is neither lost nor gained, then even in death, we continue to exist! Meaning we'll be connected forever. If you think about it, the connection we have with those who mean the most to us is a SPIRITUAL ONE! The deeper we love, the less we care about the physicality of our person. Close your eyes and focus on the word LOVE. In an instant, my mind can recreate the way my 100-year-old grandmother's voice calmed me - The joy I experienced as a child each morning my beautiful mommy awakened me. The smell of english leather still brings a tearful smile as I recall the pride on my daddy's face when I graduated from medical school. After our physical lives are over, we will always experience each other in the spiritual space if we choose to! This choice enlivens the continuation of the spiritual connection that we have always had with one another. But remember, it's YOUR CHOICE.

Right now, I invite you to take a moment and write down what memories and sensations came to mind for you. You will want to come back to these powerful memories to ground you as we walk this grief path.

If we could learn to adopt a different outlook on physical

death after creating such a sublime spiritual connection, we can learn to celebrate this creation forever. What an empowering possibility! We can choose to experience and deepen this forever connection with the person we love, even as we may be watching their physical life waste away. This proactive choice will forever transform our grief experience from something that is happening TO us – into something that really is happening FOR us and for our growth.

Throughout this book, I'll share my own personal anecdotes and tell stories of others who grieve a spouse. Whether you are on this journey yourself or are supporting someone who is, this book will provide a transparent KNOWING, a hand-holding that will help to steady you. With valuable information and tools to help you navigate this challenging time, we have each other. I pray that here, you'll find hope, healing, and a renewed sense of purpose and meaning in life that will spill over to all you touch.

And now, let's untether from the dock, unfurl our sails, and catch the wind. This moment is where your grief adventure begins.

CHAPTER 1

TERMINAL CARE

Life is a balance of holding on and letting go.
— Rumi

The last thing he ate was Häagen-Dazs Butter Pecan ice cream.

It was 2:00 a.m., and one of those nights, I just couldn't sleep. Kent was home in hospice at this point, and I was pacing my bedroom, grief-stricken. I was tearful and couldn't help but hold my breath, filled with anxious thoughts of 'the end.' On impulse, in my pajamas, I went to the store to buy the two things he loved most: chorizo & Häagen-Dazs Butter Pecan ice cream. The next day, I told him, "You know, you need to eat something," as he had eaten nothing since discharge from the hospital. I named some things I knew he liked, to which he repeatedly replied, "No." As a last resort, I hopefully said, "Well, I got Häagen-Dazs Butter Pecan ice cream," and he said, "Häagen-Dazs Butter Pecan! Oh yeah! Ya know, I love that shit!" All the family in the room cracked up! This was so typically Kent, with the best sense of humor.

He ate three scoops and died two days later.

My late husband was an upbeat, 'glass half full' kind of guy. He always encouraged me to look for the good, the light, in any situation. I felt moved to share his brightness with all who would listen – and with the thousands who fell in love with us and our journey on Facebook. After he died, I said to myself, "Well, let's look for some light in it!" The Haagen-Dazs ice cream experience continued to make me smile and was such a typical 'Kent' moment. I wanted to share it and lead our friends on an adventure that would last forever.

I also wanted to bring awareness of lung cancer to the forefront – and I wanted people to see what 'till death do us part' love looked like in real life. My goal was to compel Haagen-Dazs to change their Facebook cover photo to BUTTER PECAN before Kent's funeral – in his honor. I took to social media, making a request of all our friends and followers to change their own Facebook cover photo to Butter Pecan and to post a photo of themselves holding a carton while eating a heaping spoonful! I'm smiling just thinking of the response! You can still search the hashtag #HäagenDazsforKent and see what we did. So many folks participated! People as far away as Alaska and people that I'd never met before played this game with us! At last count, over 1,000 people were playing! At midnight on the day of his memorial service, after posts and telephone requests to their corporate office, Häagen-Dazs did indeed change their cover photo to Butter Pecan! Kent's lightness, love, and laughter reigned supreme. It still does.

During his transition, in the quietude that hospice care provides, I became present to all of the things that we created that defined US. On the morning that would become his last, he awakened refreshed, conversant, and really 'with it'! I was amazed and delighted! We recreated our usual morning ritual devotion, which we hadn't done in weeks! He raised our clasped hands from his bed and twirled me as we listened to our favorite song, "I Choose You" by Sara Bareilles:

"There was a time when I would have believed them
If they told me you could not come true
Just love's illusion
But then you found me, and everything changed
And I believe in something again

I unfold before you.
They would have strung together (I always thought she was
saying, 'We're that strong together)
The very first words of a lifelong love letter

Tell the world that we finally got it all right
I choose you
I will become yours, and you will become mine
I choose you
I choose you."

We danced and kissed. He was so alive in the moment! I think
that was the very best day of the 71 days I got to be his
wife. Wife. What a loaded word. It's weighty. It's forever.
When you become someone's wife, your definition of
yourself is forever changed. You are yoked to another on
every level. Your feelings and theirs are intertwined. You feel
their pain at the deepest level. (Even when you're mad at
them.) It is for this moment that you have been chosen!
There is a humility that spouses must take on inside a space

of confidence, "I can manage this. I can hold this with a loved one. I have what it takes to walk this journey." Remember: This isn't something that's happening TO you; it's something that's happening FOR you and for the expansion of who you know yourself to be.

As Kent's wife, I was intensely committed to keeping him focused on remembering what a great life he lived. I wanted him to die unafraid, filled with love, light, and laughter. Kent refused to talk about the statistics of survival or about his death. He was singularly focused on LIVING. Each and every day. We never talked about a funeral. I already knew what he wanted. I knew him, so I knew we couldn't communally celebrate his life in a church. I knew those things. It HAD to be all about him. I focused on making today the very best day of his life and then focused on tomorrow being even better than today and the next day being even better than that. The focus narrowed more and more to the spiritual, as everything that I knew of him in the fleshly realm faded away.

What's most important is to know and to stand for what your loved one, your spouse, wants this transition to look like – even more than what you want it to look like. I challenge you to prioritize what this experience is going to look like for them. You're taking on the care of someone and helping them to manage themselves emotionally and physically. Hell, you may have to support them in confronting the reality of their physical death. I suppose everybody doesn't have what it takes. But you're reading this book so I know you have what it takes. You want this to go well. You want to be brave. You want to be intentional for yourself and for your loved one. So, bravo to you that you are willing to be DAUNTLESS in the face of – what might be – the greatest uncertainty of your life.

Understanding the role of the caretaker is best learned through a series of questions. These questions will take place through deep conversations with your partner, as well as through some intensely self-reflective conversations. To ensure that this grief process transitions fluidly and that you experience soothing as you progress, I created a guide complementary to this book. This guide is filled with questions and provides space for you to work through the myriad transitions you'll face in your personal journey-from terminal diagnosis through the end of life. Print it out and keep it close by.

This guide holds in it four plans:
The Self-Care Plan
The (two-part) Caretaker Plan
The Terminal Care Plan

The Grief Plan

I recommend that upon diagnosis, you use these plans to help organize your journey. It will surprise you just how fast life is going to move. This diagnosis will take you on a rollercoaster of emotions and will forever change the way you experience every aspect of your life. These guides, like this book, are designed to give you focus and support to pull you through.

Scan for your FREE Guide

Let's explore these plans one by one.

The first plan is the **Self-Care Plan**, inviting you to an intimate exploration of where you are right now, how you really feel, and finding your unique ways to support yourself along this journey.

The second plan is the **Caretaker Plan**, uncovering how your partner needs care, establishing expectations, and managing disappointments. Most importantly, it establishes how to be the efficient and effective gatekeeper for all levels of care.

The third plan is the **Terminal Care Plan**, organizing transition conversations: final wishes and plans of comfort in their final days. This is critical to plan out while your loved one is able.

The final plan is the **Grief Plan**, exploring how to confront the emotions that come with grief, defining how you feel best supported, and carving a path forward.

You'll see more about each plan throughout the book. In the meantime, I need you to know that a large part of terminal care is made easier within these planned steps.

There's a sense of vulnerability inherently attached to this transition of life. The two of you will need to create a space of honesty, safety, and intimacy that will become more invaluable with each passing day. Vulnerability at this juncture is pivotal. Your vulnerability will be most effective as you provide room for your loved one to express their feelings and needs - maybe for the first time ever. This new feeling and action may be difficult for you both, but as his caretaker and gatekeeper, you must start first. In the grand scheme of everything that's going on inside of appointments and trying to maximize time together, possibly even still raising children, that vulnerability can be easy to exclude.

Kent's illness uncovered his vulnerability, and for the first time, I saw him scared, unsure, and insecure. I remember telling him once, "Just because you have cancer doesn't mean you're more important than I am." Kent was having dinner with a different friend every night. And I was like, "What about me? You're my best friend. I need time with you to unpack all this." He said to me, "Why would I want to spend even one evening with the most beautiful woman in the world talking about what? Death? Cancer? I'm not going to do it." And we never did.

I think it was too much for him. I think it was too sad for him. He did not want to discuss how I was feeling. It was too much for him to carry. Kent was a consummate caretaker. He always put me first. He would have carried what he was going through on top of how everything was affecting me. That just wouldn't have been fair.

Inside of this new sense of vulnerability, he was asking me to prioritize him, which I'd honestly, never had to do. He loved me so much and knew me so well that he gladly held my heart above his own. Now, it was my turn to do the same for him. What a lesson. It looked totally different when it became my turn. He needed me to be still with him and KNOW how much he loved me without hearing it. Humility and surrender were what was being asked of me. If you really think about it, that's what the expansion of love requires. This became invaluable because his ability to communicate lessened as the brain involvement worsened.

Assumptions and mind-reading will set you back in ways you can't imagine. So, just ask. Be direct. Create a safe space and go for it. For a more detailed list of questions, you can go to the Caretaker's Guide. But we'll start out the concept here.

How are you best comforted?
What is best for you when you're in pain?
How can I support you best when you're ill (vomiting, diarrhea, fatigue)?
When do you just not want to be touched?
Is there particular music that is comforting?
What is your SAFE WORD?

I believe in the idea of a SAFE WORD that will stop you in your tracks. The safe word exists to provide an outlet for either one of you when you don't know how to communicate your feelings. The SAFE WORD says, "Help. Stop. Listen. I need you." They use that word in a sentence, and then you know they're in a place that is so frightening that they don't even want to say it out loud. Choose an unusual word that isn't often found in a sentence. Use this discussion as a way to be honest. When exploring what your partner is most afraid of, you may be surprised to find the answer may not be death. The answer may be fear of pain, losing hair, or vomiting.

I think I missed what may have been cues because I really didn't create a space for him to fall apart. That's hard to admit. That makes me sad. I just didn't know. But you and I both know now, and we can create that space for YOUR loved one. When I think back on it, I think there were times when he just needed me. And maybe he didn't need me to say anything. He just needed me and him and quiet. Just to be close. To *feel* what was really there.

Kent said he didn't want to know any statistics. He didn't want to know what his two-year progression-free survival was. That's how they described it for lung cancer. Because he didn't want to know, even though I'm a physician, I also chose not to know. I didn't want to have data that he didn't have. That changed as time went on. As a physician, looking at it logically grounded me because I was living "out in the clouds" with him. I was "unicorns, four leaf clovers and a pot of gold at the end of the of the rainbow" with him. On one hand, I don't think there's anything wrong with staying there. But that meant that no one was going to be looking at this from a perspective of what's important from day to day. I'm glad I knew, and I'm also glad I didn't tell him because he didn't want to know. On the other hand, I do believe in miracles. For me as a doctor, "I believe in miracles," was a different statement than leprechauns and clovers and pots of gold at the end of the rainbow. It was more about meeting his expectations. I can better stand for the possibility of a miracle with my feet on the ground. Then, he could be the helium balloon with his head in the clouds with me standing firm, holding him steady. At some point, you do have to have a proactive rather than reactive conversation about when we accept what is now inevitable.

Now, I've seen people who got chemotherapy the day before they actually died. They want that last dose of chemo because they're not ready to let go. I've also seen people who get to the point where the chemo and the radiation are so painful, and the side effects are so egregious that they just really feel that it isn't worth it to continue on. Talk about that now so that as it starts to occur, you'll already know and can be the advocate.

Don't forget, as a caregiver, you're invested because this is your loved one. This is your life partner. This is your touchstone. This is your best friend, and so it's easy to want to insert yourself into their answer. Allow them to communicate completely without interrupting. Once they have said their piece without your input, then you can ask them, Do you want to hear what that looks like for me? Do you want to hear what too much would be for me? Do you want to hear? And, of course, in a perfect world, they would say yes. If they say no, can you accept that? Maybe your retort is, can we revisit it at a later date? They may not be ready to hear that from you. They may need to be in a space where *they* just need to be heard. Imagine that. For so many of us in our whole lives, no one's listening to us. And now our life is on the line. And we don't really care what anybody else thinks. We don't want the cared for to become the caregiver. Their burden is heavy enough. Really do make every attempt to prioritize them, and consider yourself after that.

Check-in with your partner on a daily basis. Maybe this happens at the end of each evening. How did today go? Are you getting what you need? Don't forget, this is a person, like most people, who won't want to ask anyone for anything. Here's this person that's ill; you're feeding them, you're making sure they take their medication, you're cleaning up after them. You're arranging their appointments and maybe still managing day to day responsibilities. You're taking on everything. They don't want ask you for anything. There's got to be an intentionality that starts with you as caregiver. Use this moment as an opportunity for you two to grow closer with that daily check-in. You're a team and must have a shared template of how things look and will work for you both going forward.

If, at the time of the diagnosis, your marriage isn't strong and you're not in a space of love, it may be a good time to explore therapy. Imagine being a terminal patient in a loveless marriage. As a physician, I've seen it happen. Imagine yourself as a caregiver in this marriage, where you don't even like each other, but you haven't pulled the trigger on divorce. Some part of you is still committed. Other parts of you may hold bitterness while living in the same house and not talking to each other. Don't be fooled. All of the resentment and hurt doesn't come tumbling out just because there's a terminal diagnosis on the table. It may be awkward and uncomfortable to care for your ill partner in the midst of this uncertainty. Here is a perfect space for you both to do some soul-searching in therapy.

An important part of your caretaker's plan will be to discuss how you will manage the expectations of the process to include disappointments. Disappointments can come in the form of treatments that show no improvement in the disease or relief from debilitating pain. You cannot get around these disappointments without having had an expectation conversation first.

In your caretaker plan, you will be able to explore together how to best handle receiving 'bad news.' Some people are deathly afraid of hospitals, clinics, and doctors. Do you know how they want you to manage that fear with them? At this moment, it is asking, how do I support you? In this particular situation that's so difficult for you, how do you feel? How do you want your doctor, your provider, to speak to you? How directly can I communicate with you? Should I be blunt? Do you need healthcare providers to speak to me first and let me talk to you about it afterwards? Create a space for that. What I found with Kent was that he wasn't even listening. It was all too overwhelming. It was my job to get all the salient information, write everything down, put everything on the calendar, and then talk to him about it.

Give your partner the respect of speaking to the doctors directly, knowing that you're in the background, writing everything down, taking note of everything, and making sure that every "I" is dotted and every "T" is crossed. There are some partners who think they want to take it all on. They might think they want to know everything; they're asking a million questions. Still, you'll need to be in the background, making sure that what is said is written down to avoid completely misinterpreting what was said to suit what they want to hear.

When you decide to stop trying to cure or arrest the disease and start talking about hospice and palliative care, it is time to look at the terminal care plan, already in place. Like, what does the memorial service looks like? Who do you want to be with you in the room when things become obviously terminal? Those are important things. These are spaces for a caretaker to honor one's wishes because, at that point, there's no talking. As much as she wants to be there, your partner might not want their stepmother in the room even if the stepmother is adamant to be there.

This part of the terminal care plan is carving out how you'll be the gatekeeper for your loved one's final desires. Kent did not believe in organized religion and, therefore, did not want his memorial to be held in a church. We had his memorial service in the Family Life Center at my mother's church, and it was overflowing. They said, "Karla, if we move to the sanctuary, people will be so much more comfortable, and we will have more space." I said, "Absolutely not. I'm here to honor him. If we move this to the sanctuary, it would prove to be a distasteful experience in honor of him." It was my responsibility, as the gatekeeper, over him and his end-of-life choices. I find that when people haven't had those conversations, they're left with, "I hope this would be what he would want," and the whole day is just a jumble of "I hope I'm doing the right thing." That's not where I want you to stand during such a time. When we have these conversations beforehand, then we can smile, then we can have a sense of contentment.

Another part of end-of-life planning that gets overlooked is the obituary. Something beautiful happened when it was time to make Kent's. I wrote it and started letting people read it and asking them to add things. They added, important things that I didn't know. You may know that he played volleyball but didn't know he was also in the drama club. So, the best friend, parents and siblings should get to read and edit it for accuracy. But then, ask them to put in one thing that defines your loved one intimately. This obituary will serve as your gift to the world, a written memoir for the rest of eternity. What's published about the life of this man, your partner, this woman you love, is alive forever.

I want to come back to the central theme that this terminal care journey is not an end but an expansion of life as we know it. The two of you going through this together will provide a deepening of connection, communication, and knowing one another—with a proactive, well-planned perspective. Don't get me wrong, this will take something. But I know you're up for it. You see the wave coming. Now, paddle out, get your rhythm, and get ready to ride to shore.

Let's Do the WORK

INTENTION

Honor your partner, yourself, your God, your loved ones and your family.

ACTION

Write down how you think your partner/spouse will answer these probing questions.

How are they around hospitals?

How do they deal with pain?

How can you best care for them when they're not physically well?

Do they desire cremation or burial?

What will they want their last moments to look like?

Be curious about how accurate you are and be willing to discuss differing answers if your partner's up to it.

Scan for your
FREE Guide

CHAPTER 2

SELF-CARE

Almost everything will work again if you unplug it for a few minutes. Even You.

-Anne LaMott

There is an aspect of this terminal care journey that almost always gets missed, neglected, and forgotten. You.

While you are completing the plans, creating magnetic connections with your loved one, and finding ways to make their last days the most amazing lived experience ever, you cannot forget to include yourself in the process.

In all of the things that need to be done, there is still you. What about you? It has been said that one cannot pour from an empty cup. Therefore, keeping your cup full will take a balanced approach as early as possible, understanding that your spouse's dependence on you is inflexible. What will you depend on with the same level of inflexibility? Here are the areas that I recommend: Look at your sense of spirituality, your relationship with others, and your relationship with yourself. Make time for personal space. I have always been so used to relying on myself – being the 'strong' one – everyone's resource. So, my advice is to connect spiritually first. How quickly and intensely you turn inward spiritually will depend on your existing practice. Be intentional about prioritizing it. Today.

This may sound like something you've heard before, but asking for these life-saving tenets to be put into place in the face of a loved one's death? Brand new.

Through this grief process, I've come to be certain that every single experience we have – especially the painful and difficult ones – exists to mature us spiritually. Get into your God space! That will look different for each of us. This spiritual calling will also move you into your friends and family space, which are both intimately spiritual connections. Evaluating where you were spiritually when all this began is the place to start. How much did you call on these entities in your regular life when a struggle happened? Asking this question now and acknowledging that a great need is coming allows you to prepare your ask in the first few weeks. Things can progress pretty quickly and without fair warning. Do yourself a favor and put into play the 'self-care plan.'

Most of us don't have one in place, so this is your chance now, right off the bat to say, "I'm going to need some help." Sure, in the beginning, you might feel as though you can handle it. Honestly, the first month - no, let's make that the first two weeks - you can probably connect the dots without reaching out for help. When I'm in trouble, I think that's probably the hardest time for me to reach out for a life line. Push through and go ahead and ask for that help from God, friends, and family.

Know who you're calling on because the ask is going to be big. To have somebody say no or not call you back can be hard, so if you've built relationships that are strong to begin with, great. If they're not so strong, then I suggest connecting with a therapist sooner rather than later. You've got to have somewhere to go with your feelings: an outlet. What I know saved me that first month was that I'd signed on for a 30-day two-mile walking challenge on Facebook. I had to get two miles in before midnight every day. That time was just for me. It gave me an excuse to get away from it all without apology or explanation. I listened to an audiobook or daily devotion, and, as a rule, I didn't talk to anyone on the phone. I gifted myself that 30 to 60 minutes every single day — and realized I needed that self-accountability to make it happen.

I needed that hour just to separate from what was going on with him. It's so easy to get sucked into that, and it can feel like a whirlpool. It can take you all the way down, and I'm telling you, looking up from the bottom is very, very, very difficult. The self-care piece keeps you floating on top of the water. So, as these waves are coming, you can take a minute to adjust your sail rather than just being completely capsized.

I think that using up some physical energy also helped me to rest at night, but that may not be for you. Not a problem! An hour of stillness and meditation, coloring, and even watching some mindless TV can help to reset and refresh — to stay on top of it all. I'm being adamant on this one, ya'll. Because it's easy to feel a little guilty taking time for yourself when this person you love is facing a challenge of this magnitude, lay the guilt aside. I'm giving you the permission you may need to choose YOU on a daily basis.

I remember one night, it was raining, and I was lacing up

my shoes at 10 p.m. to go do my walk. Kent stopped me and said, "This is nuts! What if you get sick? Can't you just sit quietly in another room in the house?" I was still determined to get out there because this was a commitment I made to myself, just for me. I deserved that time, and you do too! I said, "Look, babe, I gotta have this space for myself. You've got to trust that this is what I've chosen. This is what I need." I now realize that this 'self-care space' is sacred and must be protected as such. This need is real and your self care makes such a difference for everyone involved. Share your self-care plan with your spouse and other support systems early on. Your being refilled and replenished allows you to better care for your loved one in a balanced way.

So, let's extend this out now. What does self-care look like once we know that death is inevitable? And once they have died? If you've built a firm foundation from the beginning, I promise you that this practice will hold you in good stead through this transition. You may need more than an hour of "me-time" each day, but that sacred time will become your lifesaver through this storm. After Kent died, I really did spend a lot of time in bed being sad, and my people stayed with me – on rotation – just in case I needed them. But it's interesting. I still did do my hour in the Bible or my hour of meditation, where I just closed my door. I still did reflect and refresh during that hour of sacred, protected time. I knew I needed it. I told people, "Hey, I'm gonna close the door and give myself a minute." And I didn't feel like I needed their permission.

I truly appreciate having had people who were there looking out for me. But gosh, when you have a lot of people around, and your emotions are all over the place, it can be overwhelming. I had people wanting to sleep in the bed with me so I wouldn't be alone. We had air mattresses all over the place because so many people wanted to be on hand to help. I got a little worried that I was being a bit irritable or a bit bitchy, because people were around 24/7 at first, but then I imagined how awful it would have been if no one had been there. I apologized a lot!

For me, touch was a big piece. I had a friend who was a masseuse and did Reiki/energy work, so she was there at night to help me find calm and quiet, to ease into rest. The loneliness sometimes made it hard to sleep. It's important to know your LOVE LANGUAGE because some people don't want to be touched when they're not feeling good. Physical touch and words of affirmation are my primary love languages, and these definitely got me through those first three months after Kent died. If you're unfamiliar with Gary Chapman's 'THE FIVE LOVE LANGUAGES,' I suggest you go to www.5lovelanguages.com right now and take the brief quiz. You'll then determine whether your primary love language is Gifts, Words of Affirmation, Quality Time, Acts of Service, or Physical Touch. It's a phenomenal resource, giving you insight into how YOU best EXPERIENCE the love of others. It is invaluable in being able to connect with others, especially in times of need. Share this new information with your people in such a way that they can fill in some of the gaps that grief brings. Being able to ask for that makes a huge difference. I want you to provide a loving space for them to say, "That's all you need? I got you!"

Self-care can look different for everyone. Part of self-care is providing a space of healthy connection with others that will withstand the struggles of life. The self-care plan is foundational so you can pinpoint what you need when you're most afraid and identify the things that trigger you the most while you're in a sober mind. Maybe a trigger is feeling left out or getting the silent treatment. You can look at those things for yourself. When you are unaware of how you feel and what triggers you, it's easy to misread cues and blame your beloved for being incapable of meeting your needs. So that's where you already have a girlfriend numbers one, two, and three on speed dial. Also, this may be a great opportunity to deepen your reliance on God and "go to the throne before you go to the phone." You can be mad. You can be hurt. And you can go to that spirit-centered/universe/God place and say, "Lord, fill me," and sit there until you're filled.

I found a lot of good advice on widow-related Facebook pages. Yes. There are widow-related Facebook pages! Here's the deal: NOBODY can tell you how to grieve. People will say: "Get up early! Make your bed! Brush your teeth! Comb your hair! Take a shower! You'll feel so much better!" I gave myself permission to let the day go however the day went. No rules. No structure. I let myself feel what I was feeling and do whatever felt right in the moment. I think I went three weeks without water hitting my body. I mean, I did brush my teeth, but only because I hate that fuzzy feeling in my mouth. But that was about it. Water is a healing, powerful element. I bathed and soaked, but I did not shower. Soaking is therapeutic for me. I don't do it to cleanse my skin. I do it to cleanse my soul.

Eating seemed to be something I rewarded myself with. I found myself binging ice cream and doing things I wouldn't normally do, like heading to the 24-hour IHOP for all-you-can-eat pancakes. It tasted soooooo good. It felt soooo good. I gave myself permission to do some things just because they FELT good. And I did them without apology or inquiry. As time passed, the good feeling that pancakes brought diminished, and, at this point, I realized that I was merely numbing. It was okay at first, but then I realized I couldn't just keep going around the parts of living that DIDN'T feel good. So, instead of eating to medicate, sleeping to medicate, and working to medicate, I chose to become intentional in my choices and actions.

So, let's put a pin in your grief timeline. 30 to 45 days. 60 at the longest. I want you to be moving up and out of the pain. Looking for the sunlight through the clouds. Dancing in the rain. This proactive look at what's coming allows you to prepare yourself to limit how far down you go so that you can provide self-propelled fuel to jet yourself onto a bright future. For you all who are reading this and those 60 days have already passed, today's your day 1! Have hope. Just like all of us, you are on your own grief path.

It's crazy to think about what traditional Human Resources departments feel is an adequate assessment of how employees emote. Six weeks off for a new baby. No time off for dads because they're not 'primary caretakers.' I got two days of paid bereavement after Kent died. Two! And his cancer journey was really short – only 99 days. For many of you this process could take years. I can only imagine your level of fatigue. Suffice it to say, I was spent emotionally and physically but pulled myself together and showed up that Monday morning, anything but raring to go. As women, we know how to do this. It's modeled for us everywhere we look.

We are told to 'buck up,' to 'pull up our big girl panties,' to stop complaining, and go do what needs to be done. This, too, however, is a way of medicating. "I'll just get back to my routine, and everything will sort itself out.' I'm here to tell you, "No. It won't."

Two years later, I was completely burned out. I left my job and took six months off. Clearly, I should have had more time off sooner. I should not have gone back full-time as quickly as I did. But I didn't see any other choice. There are bills to pay and promises to keep. Grief is probably the best example of how we guilt ourselves into pushing through and completely ignoring anything that looks like self-care.

The way self-care looks for most of us is, "I do just enough for myself to be able to add more and more to my plate." Ya'll, that is not self-care. Real self-care for us who grieve provides a foundation so that when these grief memories come – like driving past his favorite restaurant – we're not completely capsized, finding ourselves again at the bottom of a quart of ice cream hiding under the covers. I had to be very intentional. I had my grief counselor, and I was still talking to my therapist every week. I was getting weekly massages and committing to daily me-time. This was life-saving! Even today, I don't step foot on the floor after my alarm goes off until I've given myself five minutes of quiet.

Like me, it may be really hard for you to empty your mind. Maybe that's not the goal. The goal is to sit with yourself and your thoughts without pushing them away for just five minutes each morning. This kept me in a good place.

So, here you are at your 30 days of 'doing it your way,' and you say to yourself, "You know what? This is feeling like I need another week." Okay. Take it. But let's hold 45 days as the threshold for moving into intention. Past that, you may be at risk for extended grief, which could morph into depression. This may require further medical assessment and medication. Friends, this is nothing to be ashamed of. Knowing yourself and giving yourself what you need without apology is the ultimate in self-love and self-care.

It's normal to look to others for comfort and solace. Remember: PEOPLE DON'T KNOW WHAT TO SAY. Just one misplaced word, and you'll turn on your heels, sliding back into isolation. I think the platitudes were the hardest for me. You know all the 'God knows best' and 'They're in a better place' phrases that people parrot. They feel like they have to say something, even though they don't have a clue what you need. So, hold back on throwing something at them. They, too, are doing the best they can. Most days, I just wanted someone to hold my hand and listen.

It's self-care to say that. "All I need today is _____."
It's also great self-care to be able to create a space where
others can ask you what you need. It's so hard when they
guess and then act on that assumption. Because then, you're
in a position of having to ask someone to stop doing
something, and feelings can be hurt. I'm giving you
permission to say when and if you just want to be alone.
That's okay. Other people might not feel comfortable with
this, but this is not their grief journey. It's yours.

In your self-care plan, you get to explore how you can
best be supported throughout this journey. Most of us don't
know what support structures comfort us the most. If you're
truly an introvert and you know that having to have a
conversation with anyone is going to make your skin crawl or
drag you into a deep depression, we need to get that down on
paper. On the other hand, if you're an extrovert and the idea
of being alone brings tears to your eyes, wouldn't it be great
to have that explicitly written – in a way that those who love
you can support you best? Although you may not want to
answer the phone, you might find it valuable to hear
voicemails or receive check-in texts at the end of each day. I
found it nice to see that someone called to check on me. If
gifts are your thing and you also would love a quick hug but
not a long visit, then your loved ones can adjust and not just
drop flowers at the door. Because it's written out, they will

know that this is you taking care of yourself while you grieve. It's not personal. Without feeling guilty or overwhelmed from dealing with compounding grief issues, you want to complete this plan in a calm state of mind. Do it sooner rather than later. This is also imperative so that people won't try to care for you in their own way and bring strife to an already tender situation.

With the best intentions, people will try to remove choice from your existence. They assume you need them to think for you. Sometimes, you may need this, but even that is hard to request. This written plan will provide all the particulars. Yes, I need meals for two weeks. Yes, I need friends to be close — but only these two friends. (This may be easier to write than to say.) No, I don't need the entire women's Bible study to camp out at my house. No, I don't need a dog-walker. Just have it all written out, so you have much less to communicate — especially when words are hard to come by.

It's interesting how many relationships are irreparably harmed during highly emotional times like this. We are hurting. We are confused, frustrated and sad. We lash out and say things we actually would otherwise never have said. We feel pushed and constrained. People are near when we need them far. This plan — thought out well in advance — can protect us from ourselves and from those relationships that are most important.

As your loved one's transition of life nears, it will be your responsibility to give all parties the opportunity to be left complete, including you. When self-care is not present, the level of your emotional intelligence lessens, and what takes precedent is you acting out of your own grief and fear. With a strong self-care plan in place, you will have the bandwidth to be able to balance your needs, the needs of your dying spouse, and the people that are most important to them.

Let's Do the WORK

INTENTION

Get to know yourself.

ACTION

Give yourself permission to take a whole day and plan to do nothing. See what comes to mind.

What does it feel like not to answer the phone?

Who did you miss talking to?

What thought/feeling kept coming to mind?

Did it surprise you that you may have found yourself in your God space?

How did that feel?

.

Scan for your
FREE Guide

CHAPTER 3

LETTING MYSELF FEEL

The only way that I can 'handle' grief, then, is the same way that I 'handle' love — by not 'handling' it. By bowing down before its power, in complete humility.

— Elizabeth Gilbert

The first experience of their physical absence is such a gut punch. My childhood wound of abandonment was amplified beyond belief. There was a vast field of darkness and even physical pain. The paradox of the need for grief while not wanting to experience it at all is confusing but is so real. My most meaningful advice at this point is to just allow yourself to wallow in it. FEEL WHATEVER YOU'RE FEELING. I believe it is this that is missing from the acceptance part of the Kubler-Ross stages of grief. It's a wailing, allowing yourself to be enveloped by and almost comforted in the expanse of pain.

As a trauma survivor, pain is so familiar to me. We all are trauma survivors; I just don't think that a lot of people are willing to acknowledge that depth of hurt. Once there is this level of acceptance, you can let yourself really feel like crap for the next month. You can let yourself grieve. I have seen people who have what's called delayed or extended grief, where it just never goes away. That's not healthy. But you do have to get to a place where you let yourself feel the awful. From there, you can start having conversations with yourself about the why, the where, and the how to move forward. I don't think you can get there if you don't just let it hit you.

This writing provides a space to let myself actually go back into what that felt like. Through this conversation I'm having here with you, I'm allowing myself to address all the stories I made up in my head in order to be able to survive. I now get to deconstruct all those tales bit by bit by bit. My childhood wounds oftentimes still leave me feeling unprotected as an adult. The death of my husband took me right back there, feeling unprotected and afraid. Now, I see that I have to be willing to have a conversation with that inner child about how sorry I am that she wasn't protected. And to remind her over and over that now I'm here to protect her. I have put supports in place – therapy and spiritual practice through healthy relationships – to make sure that I'm surrounded with protection. "Little Karla, I'm here to love you and to listen to you." I think that's a huge part of this story that is allowing me to be more and more available to myself.

Netflix came out with this blockbuster movie called 'FROM SCRATCH' with Zoe Saldana. A dear friend highly recommended it, but she didn't tell me what it was about. She didn't tell me it was a 'fall in love with the man of your dreams and they die' movie. So, I'm sitting there, watching it with my current husband. (Yes, I'm remarried!) When I realized the trajectory of the story, that the husband has cancer and is going to die, I was so triggered. Many years have passed, but still – I felt physical pain, my mouth got dry, and I heard a ringing in my ears. At that moment, I knew that PTSD was real. My husband is sitting right there. He's not touching me. I just start wailing. Screaming like a wounded animal. He said, "Babe, are you ok? Do you want to turn it off? Should I turn it off?" "No", I said through tears. "No, no, no!" He says, "What do you need? What do you need?" And I said, "I just need you to sit here with me." And I said,

"Can I tell you what I'm feeling?" He says, "Please!" I said, "It [losing Kent] was the most excruciating, devastating pain of my life, but I wouldn't have missed a second of it."

I wouldn't have missed a second. It hurt so bad, but it was so glorious. It was horrible. But the memories of it are so precious. He trusted me to clean up his vomit. He trusted me to see him in pain. He trusted me to bathe him and tie his shoes because he couldn't. He trusted me to allow him to die with dignity, surrounded by love. He trusted me to be with him in the most vulnerable, scary times of his life. I wouldn't have wanted anyone else to be there for him.

You know, sometimes I was jealous when other people were in the room. I didn't want anyone else to clean him up. If he needed to be fed, I wanted to do it. Though the experience was horrifyingly painful, I was left with this thought: What an honor to get to be the one who can hold this pain and fear and hold someone at this transition of their life. Whatever it feels like – no matter how bad it hurts, be there. Feel it all. It's the paradise of grief.

Don't let anybody try to tell you how to feel. Before it even happens, forgive them. Nobody knows what to say to you. I'll tell you what I think people need to say – "Feel however you feel." And don't try to pretend like you're not mad. But when you are mad, just be mad and tell the people who love you. Like, "I'm in a really weird place right now, where I might come off as mad, but it's not you." I think we try to hide 'the mad' for way too long.

I read this in a devotion somewhere: "The problem is that if we cannot feel the sad [or mad] feelings, we will eventually not be able to feel the happier feelings. The part in our brains responsible for sad feelings is the same part responsible for happy ones. When we shut it off, we become "Flatliners". The pain is not processed until we are willing to feel it all. Time does not heal all wounds. Even though it takes time to heal, it is not the passage of time that does the work; we need to allow mourning and crying to do their work. Some of us are unaware that we are walking around with unprocessed pain in our lives. Our lives become gray, and we think it has something to do with what we're doing, with whom we're doing it, or where we're doing it. The birth of a new life goes hand in hand with pain, as with the birth of a baby."

So this tells me that I have to feel it all. My unresolved traumas, in the face of death, define exactly what my grief is going to look like. How long it's going to last, how deep it's going to go.

I know people whose husbands died 25 years ago, and they're

still right there as if it happened yesterday. They don't allow themselves to love again. They believe that if they don't continue to feel sad, then they'll feel guilty. As if by moving on, they're disrespecting him. Let's really unpack this. Let's talk about where that connection really is stuck because it's not to the person who has passed on to the next realm. It's really a reflection of how you feel about yourself and some unresolved trauma that you've gone through. Staying stuck in the grief pit has to do with a warped sense of what love and loyalty really are.

I believe that every relationship in life is a mirror. What I'm criticizing in someone else is really what I'm criticizing in myself, amplifying my jealousies and my insecurities. So, my relationship with this person I love is going to show me myself better than anyone else without saying a word. If I bring unresolved trauma into a marriage, when this person treats me well, I'm going to bond with them even more and start to define happiness mostly by who I am with them, which sets me up for even more abandonment and pain when they die. His absence [in death] may tell me that I'm nothing without him and life is nothing without him; hence, I stay forever stuck in the grief of being widowed as the definition of who I know myself to be. If you never found a space to heal these wounds for yourself, if you attribute your healing to your husband, then your experience of grief is going to be even more horrific. Because you defined so much of yourself and your happiness in him, the source of your comfort and joy is misplaced. And I don't think that's the way we're supposed to live our lives.

You may never have had to handle something hard and painful without him. This could be more triggering than you can imagine. What if we believed that the source of the provision, protection, support, and pouring into that we got from our spouse was from God? For me, Kent was merely a conduit of God's everlasting love for me, that was there all along. What a revelation! I now understand that I was not less covered nor less loved than I was before we got his diagnosis. Even though that's exactly how I felt at first: exposed, abandoned, and alone, in that moment, the deep and instantaneous embodiment of God's love overwhelmed me. I was choked up, tearful, feeling such joy and gladness. I felt a warm energy soaring through me and visualized my heart, which had been carefully imprisoned in iron all my life; being unlocked and bursting through its chains. I can still feel it, tears spilling down my face. Now, with every beat, my heart pulls me toward pure generosity. Even if I tried, never again could I withhold love's effervescence.

Let's Do the WORK

INTENTION

Feel it. Feel it all.

ACTION

Google the' feelings wheel'. Start in the middle and choose one word that best describes where you are right now. Then, hone down on the feelings as you move outward in the circle. Sit wherever you land. Journal about what becomes present as you own your feelings.

Journal about how you tend to medicate your feelings. Don't beat yourself up. Just become aware of how you reflexly attempt to avoid feelings. (My favorite is savory foods!)

Scan for your
FREE Guide ◀ •••••••••••••••••••••••••••••••••••

CHAPTER 4

ANOTHER ITERATION OF ME

Belonging is being a part of something bigger than yourself and also having the courage to stand alone – and to belong to yourself above all else.

– Brené Brown

I hate the words, I 'lost' my husband. He's not lost. The word lost first means you don't know where something is. When it comes to death, it also means that there's a separation, that this thing is no longer yours, that he's no longer with you. I just don't believe that anymore. I know exactly where he is. What I now know is that he's wherever I am. He's with me ALWAYS. This is the first level of the new iteration of Karla. The question after Kent transitioned from this physical realm, was WHO AM I?

Because our relationship was long-distance, we lived on Skype. It felt like we were always together. We even Skype slept together. We cleaned our houses together on Skype. We meditated together on Skype. We spent 75% of our relationship magnetically attracted to one another, growing and sharing our lives – in the absence of physical contact.

I fell in love with Kent Smith so effortlessly and so completely because he touched my soul. Period. That's it. We were spirit to spirit from day one! Not only did he touch me, he truly moved me. He always said, "Everything in life is about motive. Why are you doing whatever you're doing? Out of obligation? Guilt? Tradition? Habit? If what you're doing isn't out of sincere love for yourself or for another, just don't do it."

Sigh. I can still hear his voice telling me that. I mean, It's rare to find someone who understands the nature of love like that. No one had ever cared about me like that. I'm such a know-it-all, 'smart and accomplished' blah blah blah... and he had me questioning myself! He created a space of growth, inquiry, and self-reflection, and it felt like it was just for me. I had never met anyone like him. And I just fell hopelessly in love with him. Now, I know it was really not the physical him that I fell in love with; it was his spirit.

He wrote me this amazing poem three months after our re-connection that described our love powering the planets. He said there's never been a time in the existence of the universe when we didn't love each other. I smiled at him, but I was laughing on the inside. I had no earthly idea what he was talking about. Now I do.

I gave up so much of myself to give him the level of care that he deserved. And then I remember something I chose that, to this day, still gives me pause. He was a 30-year smoker, and occasionally, while he was sick, he wanted to smoke a cigarette so badly. Gently, he would ask me for a cigarette, and I got so mad at him! I just would not let him smoke. Yeah. If I could go back and do one thing differently, I would have granted him that wish. Those days were his, and I responded to him as if they were MINE alone. That was selfish of me. I should have given that to him. I thought I was doing my wifely duty to protect him from himself, but I just couldn't handle it. The type of cancer he had genetically was proven to have been caused by his smoking. I couldn't see myself giving him something that would ultimately kill him. The truth was that, at this point, it wouldn't have made a bit of difference in the outcome of his life. I should have given him the cigarette and the lighter and then walked away and let him have his moment.

This moment for your spouse is also a pivotal moment for you. This is your first opportunity to let them go. In this small way, you are accepting what is now inevitable, and your role as caretaker begins to morph. You're standing at the door named "Widowhood." You can see it. At this moment, you intentionally place your hand on the doorknob and turn.

So, here's my takeaway for you. I saw that door and ran. I was unwilling to let him go at that moment. I was unwilling to relinquish the definition of myself as a caregiver. I couldn't even imagine who I would be after he was gone. This did me and everyone around me a disservice. Once we were in hospice, his comfort was the priority. This was my opportunity to let go. It is clear to me now that I delayed my grief process unknowingly by controlling that moment.

Here's the thing: No one can fight 100% of the time. Everyone needs a break. Just as the daily self-care time you give yourself is precious, there may be a 'guilty pleasure' that your ill loved one will request. Although we know that refined sugars, processed food, and alcohol can be inflammatory and may be unwise choices during cancer treatment, consider giving in every once in a while. Give them their favorite ice cream, french fries, or gin and tonic. When this is all over and done with, you'll be glad you did.

For you, this is where the grief plan comes in. The grief plan will transform your experience of the 'finale of death.' It's the letting go that ties back into self-care. In order to prevent being capsized by the enormity of your grief, you've got to keep pace with what you've been doing all along. I know you'll find it exhausting. As much as you can, try to get out for that walk, do that morning and evening meditation, or go to that church service. At the start of each day, be deliberate and plan out these tasks until they happen. It's weird. When this grief plan is in place with consistency, you will actually pause. For me, I wanted people to be in the house, but I didn't want them to be in my bed. I wanted them to be close by. But I didn't want them underneath me because I didn't want to have to ask anyone to leave. I really didn't want to have to call anyone to come over, either. I wanted them in the house and accessible. Describe with a clear mind how you think you might need support in the grief plan. Include also things like, who will have his ashes? Is there a place for these ashes to be shared? Who's going with you to the funeral home? If you're planning on having an actual service, who do you want to have the last view of the body?

You need to give space for that.

I remember that we asked the funeral home to come and get the body between six and seven in the evening. That gave five to six hours for people to come and just be with him. I can remember when they got ready to come take his body, I put my hand underneath him, and he was still warm. That's a beautiful memory for me: the warmth of him, still present when I knew his heart was no longer beating. That was my special time, and I allotted others the same. Make sure that your needs, which may feel intense, are met – but also provide a space for other people to get to say goodbye in their own way.

There will always be people who don't believe in your decision of aftercare (burial vs. cremation, celebration of life vs. funeral, choice of flowers/music/program, etc.), and it is not worth getting into arguments with family about that. Your job, as a spouse and life partner, is to stand firmly on whatever it was that your partner wanted – or what you feel that they would have wanted if these plans were not spelled out, as was my case. For example, people may want to honor what his mother believed. They may want a burial in the family plot that everyone else has already planned out. I've seen people give in to that, only to later feel that they've done their loved one a disservice and been disrespectful. One way of keeping the peace is to ask close family and friends what's important to them to honor their loved one, letting them know that their feelings have value – and that you can't promise, but will do your best to include their requests. Consider an association of some kind where people can give in lieu of flowers. There are many organizations that may have been important to your loved one – or are related to their cause of death – that would be thoughtful ways for them to be memorialized. I asked for donations to the American Lung Association, and we had a wonderful fundraiser for them on the one-year anniversary of Kent's death.

I remember the first shift in our relationship – the first letting go. The first necessity is to redefine myself. Once he got really sick, he intentionally distanced himself from me. Early in treatment, I remember asking him why he wasn't giving us any personal time. I said, " Babe! I need you. I'm in the crisis of my life, and I need my best friend. And that's you." He said, "You know I love you, but I can't be that person right now. I'm in the fight of my life. I've got to be a soldier over here in order to beat this thing. You're gonna have to figure it out."

I was speechless. This man had never spoken to me in that way. He was the most emotionally available person I'd ever known. He gave me everything I needed. Hearing this was frightening. Thinking back on it now, this was a gift from God because it forced me to love who I KNEW HE WAS, in spite of who I saw in front of me in the moment. He was still loving me by forcing me to rely on the TRUTH of his love rather than the FEELING of his love. This was my chance to give him back all of the love he consistently and unselfishly gave me. This is a powerful lesson that still serves me to this day, as I stand daily as this brand-new me.

It is clear to me now that this was yet another opportunity to prepare me for his absence, loosening my dependence on him. I began to intentionally walk the path of grief, having to redefine who I am in this love relationship with a man who is now fighting cancer. I was open and vulnerable. For many, vulnerability is misinterpreted as weakness. But without vulnerability, there is no space for someone to say, "Absolutely. I love you." Because until we're vulnerable, we haven't allowed those parts of ourselves that we have always felt were going to be rejected and abandoned – to be brought to light; to be chosen and accepted. This is true even in my relationship with myself! Being intentionally vulnerable means I have to pry open so many long-locked doors in my own heart and soul. Opening these doors and walking through them introduces you to even deeper iterations of yourself that you've never met.

I don't think I've yet shared with you how we found the cancer. Six months after our engagement, Kent moved to Atlanta. It was so exciting! He would be commuting weekly until things with his job were finalized. So, that Monday morning, I handed him his coffee and muffin as I drove him to the bus depot – as usual. He called me 4 hours later, saying, "Babe, something's wrong. I can't move my left hand. I can't hold my coffee cup." Thirty minutes after arrival in the ER, he called to say he had three bleeding tumors in his brain, and they were calling the neurosurgeons. They told him they thought it was metastatic cancer, but he just couldn't tell me that on the phone. I took the next flight in and rushed to the Neuro ICU, where the cancer conversation began. I was numb.

We struggled as a family. Kent was the eldest of six brothers and, as such a loving and emotionally intelligent person, was the touchstone of his entire family. He was truly beloved. And here I come, a mere 18 months into this relationship, with such a large voice in the decision-making. I get it. I really do. It was hard for them to relinquish him into my hands – and even harder to agree to his moving to Atlanta for treatment, knowing that they would miss out on what may have been the last days of his life. He needed us to be as unified as we could be. It was torture for him when we struggled to agree on a treatment. Again, I had to see the big picture – and put his contentment ahead of my being right.

For you, protect yourself, your dreams, and your family relationships. You will thank me on the other side of the diagnosis. No matter how things end, as a primary caregiver, balancing things from a bird's eye view will make all the difference in dealing with yourself and the future of family relations. Everyone comes to the same point eventually. Sometimes, it is just at different speeds. Be willing to adjust your speed, when possible, for the good of the whole family.

And when you think you're going to scream with frustration and anger, take a pregnant pause... and just breathe.

Let's Do the WORK

INTENTION

You'll never be the same. And that's a good thing.

ACTION

Believe that your person is ALWAYS with you. From this perspective, stay present and look for all the ways in a day that they are showing up. Every day, make note of something that reminds you of them. You'll surprise yourself with how much you notice they are there.

Scan for your
FREE Guide

CHAPTER 5
THE FLOW OF EXPANDED LOVE

My story will touch someone, who will touch someone else, and so on for all time.

– Unknown

A time will never exist when we don't love one another. There never has been, nor will the future ever bring, a time where our love does not exist. From the most expansive perspective, this means that I have access to Kent Smith at all times. I know – and God has been clear with me – that this is an opportunity to mature in what I know love to be. I have become the best of friends on social media with people that

I've never met. I'm talking best friends. Before Kent's death, I don't know if I could have allowed myself to deeply trust someone that I'd never seen in person. My ability to love and trust was limited by the need for physical presence and interaction. So, now, knowing he's always right here, I can call him when I want to and speak to him when I need to. Sometimes, I can hear his voice speaking in my head. Most of the time, I feel him intensely through colors or flowers or the sound of flowing water. Because I'm open to him always, any memory can bring his presence to me. It's lovely and comforting and such needed growth in this process for me. It's a vastly expanded expression of our relationship.

My advice, if you choose to remarry as a widow, is to marry someone who can love your late spouse almost as much as you do. When we were dating, I asked my husband about how much "Kent talk" was too much. His reply was so heart-warming. He told me that I'd better talk about him because there is no way that I could love him as much as I say and not need to talk about him. Now, he says he loves Kent, too, because I wouldn't be who I am for him without all I learned through this process. Check that out! What I know is this – in any meaningful relationship, you've got to be able to tell your whole story and be heard.

At the time of the diagnosis, I had a group of really good

girlfriends who scheduled weekly prayer calls with me while I was in Richmond during treatment. I loved that these women – from all different aspects of my life – created a vine of loving protection and surrounded me. I think they knew me well enough to know I'd never ask. They didn't ask if I needed them; they loved me well enough to know, and they took action. That could be a great lifeline – to know that you had scheduled weekly time to connect with the important people in your life, to help pick you up, dust you off, kiss your cheek – and send you back out there to fight another day!

Kent made a bunch of videos for me over the course of our relationship, and he'd randomly post them on Skype. At the time, I didn't think much of them, but -as you can imagine, they became precious to me afterward. So, this is something I've suggested to caretakers of terminally ill loved ones: ask them to share important memories with you – and videotape their answers. "What did you think the first time you saw me?" "When did you know you were in love with me?" "Tell me the very best vacation we ever had." "Share our very best lovemaking experience." It's so cool to watch their face their smile, and to get it on video. So when they're no longer in this physical space, you can sit with them through these videos and revel in their love for you. Watch the videos from a space of knowing their spirit will never leave you rather than from a space of their being lost to you.

Perspective makes all the difference in this grief journey!

As time passed, the phones and computers that had all these videos and voice messages broke down. I realize now that my access to these left exactly when they were supposed to. I didn't need them anymore. Because if you're holding on to things – media, personal items of your beloved - so tightly, there's no space for the universe to take those things away and create a greater space of healing.

If you are living your life and your goal and your purpose aren't to expand love, then you're merely surviving. Let's choose to thrive.

Recently, I had the opportunity to reconnect some of Kent's family. It was a profound moment, and I was touched that our story blasted throughout the internet allowed this to happen. That night, as I was driving home, I felt this torrent of love from Kent. There was this warm golden glow throughout the car, and I could feel him holding my hand – and then enfolding me in his arms. I could feel that he was so proud of me for checking my motive – and accepting myself merely as a conduit for another. It was this 'full circle' defining moment for me. I felt I had learned the lesson that he was there to teach. We are all here to help others find their way home, and this is possible when you love someone only as they are. Not the Jerry Maguire/Renee Zellweger line:

"You complete me." Though, I think that's the way that people connect to find love. We say: "There's this broken and empty space inside me. You fill it and heal it, and then I'll be okay forever!" No. That is the myth, the error. I bring my wholeness to their wholeness, and together, we expand. Our love expands us beyond the smallness of who we are as individuals in this physical realm – beyond death.

Going back to that poem, he said over and over that there was never a time in the existence of the universe when our love didn't exist. He said that our love powered planets. Imagine the vast force that this is describing. Love. Infinite. Powerful. Transcendent. Vast enough to move mountains. To power planets. To move you and I through grief.

That means that love is magnetic, that love will bring us together if we can gift ourselves and allow it to be that magnetic. Two little water droplets coalesce into an ocean of an infinite expansion of love. Water is the strongest and most flexible of the elements. It cannot be contained. It moves through the strongest rock, finding its way. Undeterred.

Grief is that strong rock. A stop sign, if you will, that will not let you pass. You have a good day, and grief says, "No, no! He's not here. Having a good day without him is not right. It's not fair to him. It is a betrayal of all that you were to one another. Come back. Hurt. Suffer. Survive." The expanded love that we're talking about transforms this boulder into a pebble and then into soft, pink sand. You know that feeling. The sand tickling your toes, making you smile as you walk along the beaches of life.

The way widowhood is depicted in the movies is one of two ways: The spinster widow in her gardening hat reminiscing her husband, long dead, as a saint and his death as the end of her life. Or, the 'bigger than life' widow who has clearly moved on with his money – his memory left in the dust. Literally.

What if this expanded love is the happiest medium that we could ever choose?

If I couldn't experience my love for Kent as being eternal inside of my current love for my husband as also being eternal, then this new idea of expanded love dies. And the myth that our only knowing of death is loss, sadness, and daily suffering remains the only choice we have. Living a fulfilled life is all that our loved ones would ever want for us. That fulfillment is impossible if we truncate the love we have – and will always have – for our deceased husband. This boulder of traditional grief becomes a wall, blocking all energies that could move us through the hurt into the glorious expansion of love.

I spoke to a widow last week after months of trying to connect. We were college classmates. As soon as she picked up the phone, in tears – she said, "Karla, How did you do this? How have you even gotten to the other side?" And I said, "It's like that, 'Going on a Lion Hunt' song in Girl Scouts! Can't go over it. You can't go under it. You can't go around it. You've got to go through it." I said, "I tried to go over it. I tried to shop it away. I tried to eat it away. I tried to rage it away. I tried to exercise it away. I tried to everything it away. I was so angry at God." That really was the first thing that I should have dealt with, but I didn't know. Now I know. So I said, "How angry are you?"

She said, "I'm so angry!"

I said, "Have you said it out loud? Have you yelled it and screamed it? And have you told God? God, what the hell are you thinking? Who does this to someone?"

She said, "I've cried so much. I can't cry anymore."

I said, "I didn't ask if you cried, right? I asked you if you've raged. "Have you just let yourself be mad?"

She starts yelling and screaming, and I'm thinking, "Yes! Go on, girl. Do it! Get that poison out of your spirit so you can move through this!"

Then I said, "I'm just gonna ask you this. Now that you've

gotten some emotions out, can you feel him in the room with you? Because I can feel him in the room with me, and I didn't know him. He's right here. Do you feel him?"

She didn't respond. So, I said, "Close your eyes. Can you hear his voice? Can you hear him singing to you at your wedding? Can you see his eyes looking at you? Can you feel him looking at you?"

And she said, "Yes."

And I said, "Can you feel his arms around you?"

"Yes."

"Can you smell him?"

"Yes."

I said. "That's because your connection with him was not physical. It was spiritual."

I said, "I want you to watch those videos."

And she says, "I do. I watch him every day."

I said, "Since now, you feel him and know he's right there. I want you to watch the videos as a conduit. Don't watch them to try to get something back that you've lost. Watch them to be present to his love for you right here and right now."

And then I said something that she said changed everything for her. I said, "God gave these men this love so that we would be there to care for them at what looked like the end of their lives. God already knew all of this when he put you guys together in college. These 40 years are a mere snap of God's fingers in the continuum of expanded love. There is literally no time between meeting them, falling in love with them, and being with them as they took their last breath! Imagine if they hadn't found us. What would that year have been like for your husband if you hadn't been there, loving him? If he hadn't had the opportunity to love you the way he did? Here are these strong men in their weakest moment, knowing they were loved. Loved in a way that ushered them into what feels to us like the end of something – without fear. Understanding that they were supremely known and chosen and loved. What an honor. You are an angel."

She said, "Mmmmm… I never thought of it that way."

She started crying.

I said, "If I hadn't gone through what I went through with Kent, then I wouldn't be here to be available to you." Now, we're holding hands, walking the pink, sandy beach, available to others to take our hands and walk out love expanded. Somebody once said, 'We are all just walking each other home.'

People don't see anything past the death. To them, it's the end of something. Now, I know that death is another transition of life. God is asking us to have a maturation of our experience of self as spirit and expansion. This flesh is so immature. It's childish. This is limiting because, as children, there are circumstances that we simply have no capacity to endure. So then, is it possible that death, the physical expiration of our body, is an opportunity for us to now expand on who we know ourselves to be?

That is the eternity. That is the expansion. That is the continuum of love that we feel for one another. It's God's love. Expanded love.

Let's Do the WORK

INTENTION

You are complete. You always have been.

ACTION

What's your boulder?

What belief is holding you as a grief hostage?

Picture it. Write it down.

Think of yourself as an angel who has come to love a hurting soul. Use the videos, messages, and material mementos to experience their love in the present, choosing to transform that boulder.

Scan for your
FREE Guide

CHAPTER 6

BECOMING PRESENT

The moment is not found by seeking it, but by ceasing escape from it.

– James Pierce

Present. Let's dig into that.

What if we can become conscious of the trauma of grief in order to transcend and become intentionally present?

Being present in the sense that I am living fully in this moment, accepting all that I am as a result of all that I've experienced. Good and bad. All of it.

I read somewhere that the definition of suffering is 'not accepting what is.' Like wishing things were different. Believing that something should never have happened. Regretting a choice made as the wrong one. Not forgiving ourselves and others when things didn't go our way. For me, it can be deeper and darker than that. My pervasive thoughts sound like this: "No matter how good you look on the outside, the bad stuff is easier to believe." "No matter how hard you try, the best in life will pass you by." I fight these feelings and thoughts daily – in all aspects of my life. So Kent's death really could have cemented these lies into my very being in such a way that I would not have emotionally survived. That would have been a travesty. I write today to protect us all from this possibility.

The sadness associated with grief in the first days surrounding the death of our person will comfort us because we're no longer holding our breath and trying to pretend this isn't happening. Inside of the sadness that will inevitably hit you on anniversaries, staying intentionally present is the goal. As time passes, this similar sadness can be capsizing because this sadness is a reaction to the memory of how bad the hurt was in that original moment. It is no longer comforting but can be destructive. These become ways of BEING that keep us stuck. They become patterns and cycles that seem to 'just happen.' That's because as we go through life's experiences, we are laying down neuronal pathways deeply seeded through chemicals and electrical stimuli. Certain triggers live in our unconscious. They run the show. This particular trigger or internal conversation begins a cascade of emotions that play out in our brains without our knowledge. Our constant limiting beliefs cause even the simplest interaction to go south. For example, a friend calls asking to borrow money AGAIN. When you've chosen to support her in the past, you were well-rested and living on the top of the hill of life's concerns. Today, you're grieving. It may be the 3-month or year anniversary of the diagnosis or the death of your person. Those disempowering conversations are running in the background, and you don't even know it. Add to the fact that you didn't sleep well, you're stressed at work, and you had an argument with your mother last night. The conversation that 'the best in life passed you by' can create a narrative that you are invisible to everyone because they just keep pulling! "Can't they see that I'm empty? I have nothing to give." And your response to your friend's financial request is filled with resentment and maybe even anger. That is not who we want to be.

Another side of these disempowering conversations is tied up in ego. Ego exists to keep you on top in the midst of stress and strife. Ego says, 'You got this. Don't listen to the BS. You can do this.' Ego doesn't understand that sometimes listening to the BS means letting go of the façade, removing the mask, and letting someone in. Another term for this would be PRIDE. Many of us have an unwritten family law that you never tell your secrets. The onion of suffering and trauma is multi-layered. By being intentionally present, knowing these triggers, and practicing self-care, we can stay ahead of and on top of these feelings.

So, stop for a second.

What is that little nagging voice whispering to you from the time you wake up in the morning to the time you go to bed at night? It might be outside of your view. So, take a minute. The best time to hear it is inside a time of intense emotion, rage, sadness, and overwhelm. I really do suggest meeting this head-on. However, you know where you are today. If now is not a good time, tuck this in your back pocket, put this on your to-do's of self-care, and give yourself a deadline to have this conversation with yourself later. I promise you will be glad you did. This has the power to transform all areas of suffering in your life, even beyond your grief. That is the power of being present.

Inside of being present, let's now discuss what this makes

available for you. What do we all want as human beings? I always say, "Life, liberty, and the pursuit of happiness."

That about sums it up, right?

Life, and having it to the fullest. That's what the Good Book says.

Life. Existence. The beating of a heart. Without a connection to spirit in ourselves and others, expanded love is impossible.

Liberty. The state of being free [in our own skin] from oppressive restrictions imposed [both internal and external] on our life and behavior.

The idea of being free seems as if it is limited to what is external. As En Vogue says, "Free your mind! And the rest will follow!"

Happiness. And its first cousin, joy, rules the day. So often, we feel that it's our outside circumstances that provide the level of goodness that we feel each day. What I know is that happiness is an inside job.

The goal: Freedom to live a life seasoned with happiness. No. Matter. What.

We have access to the fullness of life inside of our capacity to stay present. This provides the ability to transcend difficulties and disappointments without avoidance. Staying intentionally present allows us to create a safe space to inquire: "I'm off. What's going on? What am I feeling? What disempowering context has been activated?" This gives us a pregnant pause to RESPOND and not REACT.

You know that feeling when you're standing in the ocean, just a little bit offshore. You're experiencing the sparkle of the sun's reflection off the surface of the water and feeling the warmth of its rays on your skin. There again is that tickle of the sand between your toes… Bliss. And then you feel something. The sand begins to dissolve underneath your feet, and you can feel the pull of the water against your body. You turn and look out to sea and observe a wave building. You're a little too far from shore to outrun it. You're a good swimmer, but you just got your lashes done. (smile) You'd prefer not to have this wave hit you full force.

This is what our grief triggers will eventually feel like. Right now, it may feel like you're standing on the beach, and you turn suddenly and encounter a tsunami. Stay present. Feel your feelings. Use these tools. Be committed to doing the work and living the fullest, most fragrant life possible, no matter the circumstance.

Day by day, you'll remember that you're tethered to your surfboard and you know how to surf. Instinctively. You position yourself, sync yourself to the flow of the ocean, and ride that wave to shore. Eyelashes intact! (smile)

This commitment to living your best life moment by moment will hold you in good stead. I know that life doesn't always bring rainbows and sunshine and cotton candy, but when discomfort and downright grief rear their ugly heads, we can open the door and meet life on life's terms. This is only possible by living in the now with a commitment to self-love and care.

You see the door. The door that leads to widowhood and saying goodbye to the life of someone you love. When death knocks, let's position ourselves to say hello…. Preparing for a soft goodbye.

AS WE SHOULD BE

Kent Allen Pindle Smith

How can it be that eternity has kept us.
Like a meteor traveling through space.
The distance and energy we have traveled to be together,
only seems a ripple in the sands of time.
We are constant, immutable ever enjoining ourselves to one
another.
How can it be, Maisha?
It can only be because eternity exists within us.
We are eternity bound by endless, unwavering, unconditional
love.
A love which creates worlds and sets them in motion.
We are cosmic.
The power of our attraction is like gravity between planets.
Always coming together - closer and closer.
Maisha Mleta, how can it be that once 10, now 50
and still both young and ageless.
How can it be Maisha?
Answers confound gods yet between you and I, eternity is
easy.
How can it be Maisha that eternity is easy?
Because we are as we are and as we should be....perfect and
ageless.
And time and distance are no issue to eternity and love.
Love is the power and eternity is our life span.
Life bringer, Maisha Mleta, we love, therefore, we are.
We make it possible for universes to exist,
for we are eternal, boundless and powerful.
We make it possible for the sun to shine.
For it is love the conquers worlds.
God makes this possible. For God is love and life and eternal.
We are, Maisha, because we should be!

I love you, Karla. Always have. Always will.

ABOUT THE AUTHOR

Dr. Karla Booker was born in Washington DC, while her father was completing medical school at Howard University. She first dreamt of becoming a physician at the age of 11. She was raised in the San Francisco Bay Area and is the 3rd generation of her family to attend Hampton University, where she was a Pre-Med major. She is a graduate of Meharry Medical College, in Nashville, Tennessee – which is the 2nd historically black medical school in the United States.

Dr. Booker completed a residency in Obstetrics and Gynecology at Georgia Baptist Medical Center, in Atlanta – and completed her chief residency year at Saint Michael's Medical Center, in Newark, New Jersey. She practiced ObGyn for 13 years, serving as Department Chair at Southside Medical Center, the largest community health center in the Southeast. Then, in order to expand her scope of practice, she completed a second residency in Family Medicine at Morehouse School of Medicine. She was appointed Assistant Professor and Director of the Maternal-Child Health Division there. She went on to Gwinnett Medical Center, where she helped to found the Family Medicine residency program, serving as the Director of Medical Student Education, as well as Director of Maternal-Child Health. Currently she is a frontline worker, practicing Urgent Care.

Now, her favorite titles are Grandmommy, world traveler, and avid crocheter. She has 3 beloved grown children and two delightful grandsons.

Her foundational belief is that women, as the heart of the family, are also the heart of our society. Until there is diverse representation at all seats at the table and until all perspectives and input are valued, we will never fulfill our destiny as a people.